CLIMBING
any
MOUNTAIN

CLIMBING *any* MOUNTAIN

Principles for transitioning to your next level

Cherice TyRhonda Peagler

CLIMBING ANY MOUNTAIN

ISBN: 978-1-959483-97-7 (sc)

Library of Congress Control Number: 2023920241

Print information available on the last page.

rev. date: 4/22/2024

You are moving up to a new and exciting chapter of your life. This new chapter may be high school, college, a new career change, moving to a new area in the world, or committing to a new mindset. Life becomes different and a little more unpredictable and requires some adjustment. Adjustment may come in the form of making new decisions, choosing your friend group, feelings of loneliness, or having too much company and having to decide whom to keep around. I want to give you some key points to consider when making this transition. My mission is to help others walk with purpose, integrity, positive character, respect, perseverance, resilience, self-love, and discernment.

Purpose: Desires, goals, and interests that one would like to be a focus

Having a good understanding of who you are or who you would like to become is a focus that is worth your time. Just like a company has a purpose statement, you can create your own purpose statement that represents who you are specifically and what you want out of life. Your purpose statement can be as short or long as you would like it to be as you list your desires, goals, and/or interests that you would like to make your focus.

Integrity: Making a wise choice when no one is looking

Always mindful of being the same person with friends, when alone, or behind closed doors, and in public is a trait that helps you develop trust in yourself. Furthermore, others will be able to trust you if they know that you do not change based on who you are with or where you are.

Positive Character: Personality traits and behaviors that can be respected by self and others

Spend time with people who bring out the best in you, as you strive to bring out the best in others. Choose people who are good friends. Not everyone has your best interest in mind. Give others time to prove themselves before you call them friends. Feel free to leave a circle if the situation is not healthy for you. Also, feel free to stay if the situation is heathy. It is wise to model the character that you would expect another person to have, such as kindness and loyalty.

Respect: Maintaining a healthy self-esteem and acting accordingly is key. For example, treating others in a way that honors them.

Respect yourself. Even if you get off track, such is life. Refocus by positioning yourself back to your purpose. If you need to change your focus to fit who you are at a certain time, change it. Make sure that your new focus is still showing kindness to yourself and looking out for your best interest but not intentionally hurting anyone else.

Perseverance: Not giving up due to difficulties in life

Keep going. When times get tough, already have someone in place that you can talk to so you can be encouraged to move along. Also, know how to encourage yourself. Get a good understanding of what you enjoy, such as what your hobbies are and participate in those hobbies often. You will be happier if you are active in the things you enjoy. Remember not to get stuck and keep moving. Understand when you just need rest, a good meal, or to hear a favorite song to help you get your second wind to get you back on track. You can do difficult things. Even if you make slow progress, it is still progress. Delayed does not mean denied. Run your own race.

Cherice TyRhonda Peagler

Resilience: Recovering from life's challenges

Perseverance and resilience encourage a person not to get stuck in a challenge. The difference between perseverance and resilience is perseverance is more goal focused on putting in the work to accomplish a difficult task. Resilience is the ability to remain balanced or grounded after something has interrupted your life for the worse. Through trial and error, try a different method to achieve your goal. If something does not work out, you will discover what does not work for you or what you do not want to do. Being able to maintain a healthy mindset during and after adversity is a sign of resilience.

Self-love: Accepting self and showing action to take care of self physically and emotionally

Care about yourself enough to focus on what matters to you. Identify those interests and hobbies that you love, and give those things your attention. Be mindful of what you need at any given time to be able to sustain your best self. Unlike the love from others, self-love is always available.

Discernment: The ability to decide well

Knowing when to say yes or no to a situation is going to save you time and energy. When you do not know the answer to a question, it is okay to ask for more time to think about the situation. Do not allow someone to push you into making a decision that will cause you to lose sleep, give you anxiety, or move you into depression. It is okay to say "I'm good for now." If something is meant to happen for you in the future, you can say yes to it in the future if that is what you want then. If you say no to something, then understand why you are saying no. This way, you can remind yourself if the time comes when you are uncertain of why you made a certain decision. Seek results that lead to peace, feeling good about yourself, and sleeping well after making the decision. Respecting yourself and others in the decision process is a way to show that you care for yourself and others. Do not be afraid to consult with someone you trust to figure out your best decision.

Just some thoughts (A–Z) to take with you just in case you only have time to read a list:

Apply what you know and grow from there.

Be aware that emotions are energy in motion. Ride the wave until the motion becomes level again.

Create a healthy life.

Delayed does not mean denied. Remember this.

Experience is a teacher. Learn from those experiences.

Focus on the positive, but have a plan to remove the negative.

Go for what you know.

Help yourself by loving yourself.

Ignite your growth by continuing to learn.

Joke around when something is funny. Humor is healthy.

Keep others around who offer helpful perspectives.

Leave behind worries that you have already processed and have taken you as far as they can carry you.

Make a list of healthy coping skills for when things get tough. When needed, pull out those coping skills.

No is a valid answer. Honor your boundaries. When you say yes, let that yes be a light to you and others.

Options may come slowly. Be patient for your best options so that you can make the best choice for you.

Pay attention to whether someone is having a conversation to lift you up. Any other reason is unproductive.

Quit when your intuition tells you that you are done. Avoid the unhealthy repetitive cycle.

Realize what you need to feel safe. Make that need a requirement.

Staggering to get up is okay. Just keep rising.

Talk about your deeper feelings that need healing to a trusted person. You can heal when those emotions have somewhere to go other than your head.

Utilize your identified strengths.

Visualize what you desire and use this as a blueprint. Make changes when needed.

Work with integrity and purpose.

X out distractions.

Your best self is when you can feel good about your choices.

Zoom in on the beauty of life. What you notice is subjective. Take the beauty that you notice even if it is only a glimpse of beauty.

Summary:

Climbing Any Mountain is a daily guide for the reader who desires words of affirmations as a tool to manage day-to-day challenges that arise. Climbing Any Mountain will serve as a reading companion for a reader to understand that life challenges are universal. We can strive to overcome challenging thoughts, maintain a healthy mindset, and exceed limited personal expectations with a mindset that encourages self.

www.ingramcontent.com/pod-product-compliance
Lightning Source LLC
Chambersburg PA
CBHW070958120626
46546CB00004B/1677